Because...

Tasia Marie

DEDICATION

This book is dedicated to a woman who taught me
how to be strong. She taught me how to be me,
and there was never enough time to say thank
you for all she did..
R.I.P Sheila Medina

ACKNOWLEDGMENTS

Thank you, to my Family, and close friends, who helped me reach my goal of finishing this book.

And

Thank you to all the people who inspired these poems
Without you, I would have never broken, and learned how to put myself back together again...

And you can become
Everything your heart
Desires...

Because
Even if I can't see
The beauty in myself
I can see it in you
And I believe
That's enough
To keep me
Holding on...

Because

You ignore
My blood spattered flesh
Because
It frightens you
Because even though it stains mine
You believe
My blood is on your hands...

When I'm with you
Those neon lights
Seem dull
Even
In the middle of the night
Because
You shine brighter
Then any love
I've had before...

Because
Stars shined
And blinded my eyes
When you said
You loved me...
But
Galaxies
Exploded
When you said
You never did...
And at first
I thought
It was the end
But baby
Little did I know
Life comes
From Catastrophic events...

I left because
It was my time.
Your soul wasn't
The only one
That needed
Saving...

Because

I question what love is
And that's not entirely
Your fault
I had to love
And have had loss
So I could know
What's true
And
What's not...

Your voice
Somehow numbed my pain
And at first I was
Slightly scared
But then
I turned my fear into
Adrenaline
But I've come to realize
That everyone should be scared of something
Because even the things
That take the pain away
Can bring the darkest
Cloud into your life...

Because

Begging you to stay
Is what tore me apart,
Because I never thought
You'd chose
Something else over me
And the realization of it
Sent me into my own personal hell...

All I wanted was to be loved
And it's gotten to the point
Where I don't even think
I'd mind
Toxic love....

I wanted you to beg me
I wanted you to fight for me
Because all I wanted was to stay...

And you never even asked me to.

Because love was
Carving
Your name
Into a tree
And coming back
5 years later to realize that
Just like trees
Love can let its roots
Grow deeper
Or wither and die...

Because

I wonder if
These people
Have lasted so beautifully
And perfect
As their names
That are etched
So carefully
Into these trees...

And I hate how
As I sit here
In nothing but peace and serenity
I feel darkness lurking
Just in reach because
Just as everything
That allows you to see beauty
And to feel happiness
It must come to an end....

Because

Because I feel more lost then I am found,

And I'm drowning in my own sadness...

Those foreign
Beings we all
Dream of
Will never
Take us away from this hell
Because
They're even scared
To fall in love
With beautiful things that die...

Something deep inside was
Dying to get out
Anyway it could
Because all it wanted
Was to be away from all the pain
He put it in...

Despite her beautiful flawless skin
She knew she'd never
Keep her innocence
Because her horns
Were now dark and twisted
And it was time for her
To live in sin...

Because

Because the sun was setting
And I looked up and realized,

You weren't the beautiful one...

I was...

Because
I want things
That never want me
They always seem to
Leave me behind
Because I'm
Not good enough
For You or Death...

Because

You came and covered
Me in darkness

But to everyone
You were beautiful

You were always the focus
And for awhile

Everyone forgot

What you had covered up
And I could no longer shine

Because baby,
You were my eclipse...

And I'm at peace
With the idea
Of you
Changing me
Because I know
You're too good
For me
And it'll only
Be for
The better...

Because

When I look back
I don't know
Who the hell
I wrote some of these for
Because
I called you perfect,
But then I should have known
Nothing stays perfect forever...

The TV's not on
I don't think I want it to be,

Because before
I fall asleep
I'll let
My demons
Speak...

Because I think you'd like
2pm me
But 2 am me
would frighten you,
and 4 am me...

.

.

.

.

.

.

.

.

.

.

.

.

.

.

.

would make you
never come back...

I crave to feel
Safe and loved
I crave a home
But I'm not very sanguine
About finding one
Because I make people I love
My home
And every time
They leave
I'm left
Emotionally
Homeless...

Because

I fell in love with moments
But that won't help
Because
You were
All of my greatest...

Because
Losing sleep
Is worth
Making sure
I have you
When I do
Wake up
Tomorrow...

Because in this
Dark world
I've made
My bed in
You're the only light
That's not dim
You're perfectly happy
Cause
You're everything
I need...

When I can't sleep
I want you

To drive to my house
At 2:36 am

Because

You wanna
Play video games

Listen to music
Give me hugs

And make me forget
What sleep is...

Because

They use me
Like some
Disposable camera
It's perfect for the moment
But then once the pictures
Are developed
It's no longer
Desired or usable...

I wish
Time reversed

Because
You are hers

Because
I found you too late

Because
I realized

You were the boy
I wanted to fall for...

Because

You can be so happy
And it bothers me
Actually
It gets under my skin
How someone
As imperfect as you
Can be happy
And me?
I'm more pathetic
Than ever...

You're simply
Perfect
Which is hard
To accomplish
Since
I swore there
Was no such thing.
Because love
Has been more than unkind
But I'm willing to
Take back everything
And admit
You're perfect...

Because

And because
For years
I wished to feel
Nothing.
To be numb,
And all at once
It came true

And then I realized
Why people
Should be careful
For what they wish for...

And it's
Not settling
It's finally
Being able to
Be content
To learn to be happy
Not with others
But with myself...

Because allowing
People to see
That I'm dying inside
Was never an option.
Instead it was a shock
When I finally
Admitted out loud
How much I wanted
To die...

Those clouds
So blue
As we flew
To our
Neverland
Forgot to warn me
That sometimes
Never growing up
Is detrimental
And that happily ever after
Is over rated
Because
Not everyone gets their fairytale...

Because
When I looked
Down
At my reflection
I realized
I shouldn't be staring
Into the puddles
My tears had made
But instead
Have been staring
Into eyes
That reflected
Nothing but
Pure
Happiness and Beauty...

I'm tired
Of those boys
Who only behind
Closed doors
Can genuinely
Be
My kind
Of perfect...

Because

These monsters in me
Beg to surface
And I fight them knowing
No one can love
Something as dark as that...
But you, you were different
You found
Reckless endangerment
Attractive
And at first I thought
We shared a love for darkness
But then I realized
You were the monsters and darkness
All in one,
You were all my evils combined
You were my end...

Because you can stitch close your veins
And watch the scars begin to heal
But the feelings inside won't fade
You'll never forget
How he made you feel...

Because
Sometimes I believe
That all that pain
Was better
Then how I feel now
Numb and not alive...

It took me all this time
To realize
That it wasn't you
I was in love with.

I was in love with
A feeling
A place
Our Nirvana...

Because

All I want
Is to feel
Deeply,
Without
The hesitation
In fear
Of
Rejection...

You're telling me
That in this time
I've learned
That sometimes
We don't want to love
But we do
In fear
Of the things
We may just miss...

Because

And you stole something
I'll never get back,

My ability
To love without
Hesitation...

Because at 6 am
In this empty bed
This is what it feels like
To know
That she's happy
You are in hers...

You don't even know
That I know
    Your eyes dance
    When you're lying
      It's because
      I looked into them
        Hoping for you
        To save me...

Every time you lied...

I was less than ready
To realize
I'd never be free
Because when you owe
Your life isn't yours
And it never will be
Because
All people know how to do
Is take, take, take
And all you've been taught
Is to give,
Till there's nothing left...

Because

Incinerate
What's left
I promise
There won't be
Too much smoke,
There's not much left...

There isn't enough
Love to fix me...

You made me believe
In something
I knew wasn't real
You gave me magic
At a magic show
Yet you weren't the magician
You were planted in the audience
You were a stranger
Who was only
Apart of the show
You were only a part of the illusion
Never meant to stay,
And now as the magic leaves
So must you...

Love;
That time stamp
On the clock
Reminds you
You're waiting.
Waiting for something
You're not even sure
You believe in...

Because

Those shades of blue
Never seemed so beautiful
Till it was all that consumed me
And now I can finally
See the beauty
In the sadness
Of letting go...

I never asked for much
Except for you to love me
Love me,
Because I loved you
Like the night loves the moon
Because without it
It'd be left in darkness...

Because

These feelings
Of inadequacy
Are buried so deep
I doubt
I'll ever experience
The joy
Of being content...

You envisioned a world
As beautiful as can be,
But little did you know
You'd never be set free...

I didn't know why
You fell just as fast
And I was scared
Because that's what happens
When you're a love addict;

A person who loves
Limitlessly
And who crashed and burns
Alone...

They told me there
Are no heroes
Because everyone
Is too busy saving themselves
I'm not looking for a hero
I'm merely looking
For someone
To simply
Give me a little of themselves...

Because

Your fingertips danced across my skin
Letting me forget those
Colorful words you yelled at me
Allowing me to remember
The beauty inside
That I was unsure
Was even there...

You've left me
Overwhelmed
Drowning in
2ft of water
And for
Some reason
I can't seem to
Simply stand up
&
Save myself...

Because

So I'll ask you how the future is
And you'll say, just fine
But it saddens me a little
Knowing your future
Will never meet mine...

Lost in thought
Of what could be
Infatuated with a
Memory of a future
That may not be
Captivated by your
Words and Promises
To set me free
These hopes
Enticed me
To give into everything
A foolish tale,
Is what I've become.
Giving things that
Should be earned
A worthless girl
With meaningless hopes
Love has become a common lie
Something she only dreams
Of finding in life...

Because

I am a human being
And you've painted me a shadow
That lives a better life then I.
You don't even see it and it gets more
Attention then I
It receives more praise
Than I.
I am a human being
Who longs to be
My own shadow...

These memories
Never seem so faded
I waited for them to appear
Only realizing
You can't make sense
Out of the surreal...

There isn't a single
Thing

Someone could tell
Me

To make me
Believe

That everything is going to be
Okay...

Because it's all you know...
You can't fight
The urge
To be scared,
Or
The urge to run
From a love
That is anything but toxic...

Because

I can't understand
How someone
You love
Is capable
Of allowing
One of your greatest fears
To become reality...

My rattled mind
Can't find the words
To describe
The way I feel
Because
Love and Hate
Can't combine
To form
Forgiveness...

Because

These idiosyncrasies we fall back into, Take
What little independence
You claim of your own, Threatening
Our very sanity, Questioning
If we were ever right, Wondering
If we ever truly knew what love was...

The nights are colder
As is this love
It's dwindling like a fire in the night
Just as dark hits
It shines brighter than we ever imagined
And now as the night has carried on
The light begins to die
We don't bother feeding it anymore
We're too busy fighting
We're going to let it die
But instead of letting it
Die on its own
You smothered it
And put an end to it
You killed this fire...
You ended you and me...

Because

This is the sadness
That lets me write
Those dark words
That never see light...

I'm so scared of being without you
I'm scared
That I'll slip
Back
Far back
Into
Reoccurring fatalities...

Because

The colors you've etched
Across my sky
    Have shown me beauty
    Is hidden
        Even at the end of the day...

        When there's nothing left
        But our sunset...

You break me
Every time
I'm happy
And all you can say
Is fine...

Because

I'm holding your hand
A bit too tight
I need to let go
To see
If you want to fly...

You've taught me
The most important thing of all
I don't need love to be happy...
I need to be happy
In order to actually love...

Because

I'm tired of these
Twisted tales
These endings sounded better
In fairytales...

There's this attractiveness
To forgetfulness
Like yes, I forgot to worry,
Yes, I forgot to feel sad...
And yes...

I forgot to love
Things
That don't love
Me...

You're searching
For the light in the darkest
Parts of your mind.
So I ask you
To please let me
Help you find
The beauty inside
The hope of brighter days
And most importantly
Show you
That I believe
You can get through this...

So cold
And distant
You play it so well
Or maybe this is you
Being comfortable
And forgetting
What love is...

Because

And it's over
You've lost the one person
Who is still alive,
And capable of
Loving something
Like you
Good job
You piece of shit
I hope you die tonight
At least
No one will miss you...

It's 4am
And my thoughts
Beat at my minds doors
Begging to be let in
And heard
They are not the kind ones
That reassure me of love
They are the ones that rip
My poorly sewn seems
To shreds
Reminding me
Love is never
A good foundation
For anything...

Because

I pray to a god I don't believe in
Every day for an easy way out
And then I wake up and
Realize I'm going to
Have to do it
Myself...

There are no words
When all that's left is to cry
I'm literally loosing
Every fragment
Of sanity left in me
And all I can fathom
Is why I am not enough?

Because

Maybe when you
Think about
Opening the car door
When it's going 65
Then maybe, just maybe
You'll understand my thoughts...

Finishing something is the hardest thing to do. Finishing a sentence by finding the right words. Finishing a letter that will be reread and picked apart trying to find more than what's written. But the one that may be the hardest is finishing life, realizing that its time, that this is no longer what is expected. People say you need two things in life to survive, Love and Faith. I've never had faith before, so love, looking for love is what I did. And I found it and invested it in places it never need be. Then I thought I found it, the true love. Thought it was going to prove that happiness is real, and that it can be felt for periods longer than a moment. Unfortunately, moments of happiness do not drown out a life without it. That moment is flickering, fading, never to shine bright again. With that comes my time. I can't live this unhappy. Ask me a feeling, ask me an emotion. I'll say I'm sad because it's the easiest way to describe me. Yet there's so much more to it. I loved you, and always will. Always. I want and need you to be happy. You will find someone better than me. You all will, I promise you. I'm sorry, for all the pain I am about to cause you...

Because

This faint heartbeat
That beats from your
Pale skin
Is unfamiliar
In so many ways...

Slit your wrists and see how much you feel then...

Anger and Sadness
Are drugs
Take a deep breath
Blow out
Feel dizzy as carbon
Leaves your body
Breathe in
The foreign pathogens
Sickness in every breath
Madness in every breath
Your sanity was never
Welcome Here Anyway...

He makes you ugly
He makes you question
Those little things
Those tiny kisses
Those short hugs
Those brief hand rubs
He makes you ugly
Because you let him
Erase who you were
Even though he makes you ugly
You're still so damn radiant...

Because

Your looking
Glass
Is too filled with
Smoke.
Stop trying to
Predict
A future not yet
Yours...

What I want is
All of you
What I need is
Your love...
So I compromise...

For now...

Because

No one said
The Queen of Hearts
Actually had to
Have one...

People ask
Why
She would ever want to be a star?
She simply replies
Those stars
That I aspire
So hard to be
Are burnt out and dead...
And yet people
Gaze at them
In awe of their beauty...

You are the reason I cry
But you are also the reason I smile
In every bunch of sweet strawberries
There's always a sour one
Not all moments can be beautiful
For then nothing would be special
You are my reason for holding my breath
I can't figure out which one means more...
I'm hoping you'll keep me breathing for a little
while longer...

That moment when you realize
The sky is blue
Sometimes the grass is green
And
Not everything in life is meant to work out...

Because

I swear on my life I hate everything about you...
I hate who you are
What you do
And how you act
You disgust me
And everyday
I wish you were dead...
Because I'd be just fine without you
I really would
Just some of the benefits are good
But I still wish you were dead...

The unsteadiness of these thoughts
That flutter deep within my mind
Have caused me nothing but pain.
Heartache and pain
That's mostly self inflicted
Reaching out
Was never an option
For I am not crazy
I will not be the pill addicted fool
Even though sometimes
Pills became appealing.
Somewhere along this journey
I've lost what I once believed
And now
All I simply do
Is want to feel free,
And I believe that it's worth it
At any cost...

Because

Discarded
Tattered and Torn
Left mangled by
What little you knew
And little you know
About a bond that we once shared
Your actions left me to wonder
Were you ever really there?

So in sync
Yet so distinct
In the things you've
Become to do.
This turmoil
Dwelling and stirring
Deep within
Can be what makes us
So discorded...

You're forgetting
Your words
That were filled with promises

You're forgetting
My love
Filled with forever's

You've left me
Alone
I've fallen behind

You've forgotten
The we
Replaced with I...

These distancing
Words
Grant me the power
To close my eyes
And validate my pain...

These feelings are familiar
Yet so foreign at the same time
My mind still too filled with
Little lies
The effort is there
With effortless care
I question is
How I make you feel fair?
Lost and delirious
Is my heart
Confused and mysterious
Are my feelings in the dark
I close my eyes
And all I see is you
When I open them
I should see me too...

I'll search for the missing pieces
When I know you have the parts
I'll question myself again
When it's simply a matter of the heart
The memories incinerate
Like fire on a cold winter day
The air is filled with silence
For there is nothing left to say...

Because

Trust is something gained
Not something that's simply granted
But be wise
With secrets you tell for
Judgment will unconsciously be bestowed
Regardless of love
Regardless of bonds
My mouth may say that's okay and fine
But my heart will always feel otherwise...

Anger spewing
Inside
Laughing
Because it holds back the
tears
More than done
And it kills me inside...

Because

Sometimes I feel my heart
Sink so deep down
I don't think it's ever coming back
And honestly
I wouldn't mind if it didn't...

She pleaded to gods
She didn't believe in
Begging to simply be happy
But even in her darkest hours
Her soul
Left her to die...

Because

In the midst of the night
When the wind questions me
I'll remind her
She only reminds me
Of the cold in
Loneliness...

I wonder if your love
Is something I'll remember?
But then again
With that question alone
I jeopardize everything
I'm clinging on to...

Because

These things
May be small
But they
Have large
Rippling effects...

Those moments
You take
What I no longer can
Give
Are the moments
That test
My strength
The most...

Because

I was happy...

And in an instance
The memory
Rushes in
And I remember
The hate
And it overwhelms
What little happiness I have left inside
Till there's nothing left
And the hate feeds
On my soul
Which festers
Into self worthlessness...

He reminded her
Of better times.
A time
Of happiness
He held hope
And a future in his eyes
But soon
A shade of grey
Covered his eyes
And a comatose
Death stare replaced
The beauty
And now when she stares
Begging to see
The happiness
From better times
She sees darkness
That jilts away
The very essence
That captivated her...

Sinking
Falling deeper and
deeper
Into a forbidden
Madness
That many
Call Love...

Because

Little things under my skin
Keep biting and nipping at me
Little things under my skin
Like constant sharp needles or pins
Little things under my skin
Anger me, when they shouldn't
But
Little things under my skin
Can make me
Rip myself apart
From within...

There are times
When I remember
A dream
That for some reason
Seems more and more
Like a memory...

When words are spoken
It's too late
To reverse
The tragic
Outcome
Especially
When its
Coming
From someone
You love
That they
Irrevocably
Regret
Adopting you...

I need to take
And turn
How you make me feel
Into words
Into beautiful words
That trap my feelings
And expose them to
Others
For if I don't
Or if the words
Are not
As beautiful as they should be
I am as worthless
As I thought...

You're loosing
The only girl
Who will ever love you
Despite your flaws
Because she sees them
As why you're so
P e r f e c t

We may realize
When it's too late
That our hearts
Don't beat
As one...

Because

You wonder
How could
A girl
That beautiful
Destroy herself?

She's simply
Fighting her
Monsters
To stay alive...

These cuts
Are merely
Surfaced demons
That needed to bleed.
You can't feel the pain I'm in
But you can see it,
You can see them...

Because

It's like 3 am
And I'm still waiting
For you call
You trick me every time
Your dumb but,
I'm dumber
Cause I'm the one
Who falls...

I'm remembering everyday
That things change
You said things
I wish you never had
I love you
And I wish I didn't
I miss you,
But I'm going to remember
That this
Is not something worth
Chasing...

Because

You remind me
Of better times
When things
Weren't so dim
And I could
Still see the light...

Let me condemn myself to purgatory
Drowning myself in a erroneous desire
Let this affliction
Feed my monstrous soul
This exceptional happiness
I've seemed to machinate
In this insouciance for my own life
I've let despair devour
The most esoteric
Parts of my mind
What's left is a futile soul
With the ability to be used and abandoned
You need tattered souls
So that the pure ones
Are left untouched
So I'll find importance
In this misconstrued utopia
Living until
Emptiness is no longer enough...

Because

The same love songs
That made me think of you
Now leave me
Emotionless...

Faking happy
Something I've grown quite
Good at
If only
You could see into my eyes
Into my burning soul
I'm screaming louder than ever
And every day
I say
I just can't take it anymore...

Because

I allowed you
To eat away
At what little
Innocence I had left
But with that
You've managed
To kill
This love
I had for you
So thank you
For hurting me
Making me feel
Worthless
Thank you
For being
Exactly
What you said
You'd never be...

I beg
Of you
To take me
Away
Far away
To save me
Before
I destruct
Because I believe
There's life after death
Most importantly
Happiness
After death
So profusely
I beg you
Please don't let me
Save myself...

Because

This soul incinerates itself
From the inside out
Burning, slowly dying
A slow and painful death.
Then decaying
For no one cares
To ease this soul to peace
So even after death
It was never good enough
To be happy...

Out there is hope
Out there is you
There you are
So wholesome
So safe and strong
And here I am
So broken and weak
I'm not your project
Don't fix me
Just love me
For awhile
Help me
Heal myself
Show me
The things
I've missed
The moments
I've only dreamed of
Show me how you love me
Help me see
Things right
For the first time
Open my eyes
To the things
I've missed
Just simply love me
For awhile...

The things you've done
Are disgrace worthy
Reminiscing on a past
That's better left forgotten
Holding old feelings and thoughts
Closer to your heart
Then the ones that mater now
Disgraceful thoughts
Turned into displeasing actions
Letting yourself betray
A commitment
You deserve
Your scars
And
Your new found ones
You are
A disgusting disgraceful soul
And peace
Is something you'll never find...

I think I'm scared,
Scared of feeling again
You've come along and
brought
Such feeling and destruction
Into my life
I self destruct with the
Thought of pain
Only to inflict it upon myself
You hurt me
While you only mean
To save me...

The drift begins
Our once conjoined hands
Begin to slip
You're leaving me
Slowly but surely
You'll realize it
I can see it now
But I'll hold on
Letting you be the one
That ends it all...

And in all my dreams
I repeat the same thing
"It was nice knowing you"
Like I'm off to
Some place
I've never been...

Because

And the calling of pain
Never felt so
Heart warming
I can't make you love me
I never wanted to
But since I'm not perfect
I'll make myself
A little more
Uglier for you...

Maybe
If your fingers
Could cut her
She'd yearn
For your touch
Like she does her blade...

Because

Have you ever believed
That you are single handedly
Responsible
For annihilating
Someone's
Happiness...
While struggling
To remember
Your own...

Somewhere along the way
I lost you...

Because

My hand is unsteady
Waiting for what seems to never come
The happiness may be there
But I count the seconds till it's gone...

I know why you stay
You don't want my blood
On your hands
So here I will promise you something
Leave
You are not worth the
Cuts of a blade
The pain
The ridicule
The dirty looks
You were worth
The time
The love
You held
My hopes and dreams
But you are not worth
The cuts and the pain...

Because

I'm scared that I will take my own life
Fearing that I can't handle the little things in life
That seem too overwhelming
What am I to do?
When the little things you do
Make me feel so unwanted
I understand it's a lot of faith
That I've placed in one person
But without you
I will be
No more...

You don't get it
When I say
I love you more
It's because I do
It's because
Everyday
I kill myself
A little more
Because the pain inside
Will never see
The light of day
In fear
Of loosing
You...

Because

I remember when the tears use to fall
Because the rain never came
Now the tears fall
Because the rain comes too often
The darkness has clouded
What little light
I had left in me
The destruction
That I cause myself
Is devastating
And as in every storm
There will be
Fatalities...

It's like I can feel it
In the pit of my stomach
That feeling
Of emptiness
When it's caused
By you
Tormenting
Your own soul
Due to the
Numbness you feel
Everyday...

Because

And I can honestly tell
The exact moment
You fell out
Of Love
With me...

My reasons
For why
Are diminishing
Fading
Never to be
Called upon again
So I let
The darkness swallow me
We both knew
That my absence
From this madness
Would only
Last awhile...

Because

A distant love
Of a hand
Running across a page
Of feelings
Escaping a soul
That feels forgotten
Remembering the happiness
That's harder to find...

As you sleep
I wonder
If I can do it anymore
To disguise
Pain and hurt
To not
Only you
But to myself
As something
Less significant
That breathtaking
Talent is slipping.
I wonder why
I bother using it
But then
I remember
If you saw
How I really
Felt
You'd run
So far
Screaming she's Mad
Cause sometimes
The monsters
Inside
Almost
Scare
The life
Out of
Me...

Because

I feel so disgusted
So empty inside
I'm not good enough?
I no longer make you happy?
I can feel it
In the pit of my stomach
That maybe
This isn't
Going to
Work...

I'm broken
Every time
Your eyes look at me
I brake a little more
Knowing
You hate me
Knowing
Every day you fall
More and more
Out of love
With me
It kills me
Just as I am planning
On doing
To myself...

Because

I start crying and you ask me why,
Is this some sick childish game to you?
Feelings never mattered
Or maybe yours to much
Letting mine get lost in space
Never to be found again
I love, I feel, I miss things too
But if what I want in life isn't good for "us"
Tell me
Because once again you'll prove
That I was never good enough...

I sat there staring at him. Waiting, for his lips to move, but they never did, they never even quivered. The whole time I sat there I wasn't hesitant of what you would say. I was scared of the silence that now left me alone...

Because

It's like everyday
I fail at your Perfect
Living in my own world
You've caught me
Spinning my own web
Of lies
I'm happy
I'm okay
It'll get better...

I don't know
If you know
What it's like
To be
A person
Who's
So filled with darkness
The light in you
Hurts my eyes...

Because I don't
Believe in God
But you got me
Praying that death
Treats you the
Way you treated
My love...

You were the light
In the black hole
That you placed me in...

Because

Take me
somewhere
I can make wishes
On shooting
Stars...

Even though
Its 2 am
I don't feel alone.
I'm unfamiliar
With this
Because for once
I am not loved
By others
But finally
By myself...

Because

That long walk
Where I heard
My ghosts
Whisper
You're better off
Dead...
And as those
Branches reached out
And cut my arms
Almost effortlessly
I believed them...

I wanted to be
Someone
You wished for
Because
We as lovers
Only wish
For things
We think are
Beautiful
&
Extraordinary

Because pain is temporary
They say,
Well sometimes
I wonder
What it's like
To be
Happy...

You were simply
That addiction
I could not quit
You made me
Mentally sick
And unstable
Yet somehow
I perceived it worth it
Because
You made me feel
Loved
And that's
The worst
Addiction of all...

Because these
Words
Were never about you
You conceited shit
They were about
How I felt
Every time
I died
Inside

I believe
Everyone has
words
That are so
Deep seeded
Into their souls
That speaking
them
Would shatter
Their very
essence...

During that drive
Along that windy road
I feared we would crash
Because
You stared
Longingly at those
Beautiful stars
That shined
Bright Beyond
Our reach
And then
I realized
That I was just
A passenger
In this car,
Not a loved one
Not your loved one
And more specifically
Not your stars....

How do you tell someone
They can't love?
Because everyone
Who's loved me
Has hurt me,
And I can't bare the idea
Of you hurting me too...

Because

Your hands
On my body
Repulse me
Because I remember
When they were once

Not So Kind...

And then you'll be gone, like everyone else.
Just like everyone else who made me temporary
In their perfect existence...

It's Funny

Because

You're everything

You say you're not

And I fucking hate

Every inch of you for it...

You remind me
That Failure
Will always be
My Biggest
Success...

Because

One day
Someone
Will take
All this sadness
And let me
Be Free...

And I thank
A God
I don't believe in
That you weren't
My end
Because for awhile
I thought
You were...

Your love
Was like the roses
That grow in spring
It grew from darkness
And at first they were
Beautiful
But then the thorns
Began to prick my
fingers
And your petals
Began to fall
And then I realized
That your love
Just as these roses
Has wilted,
And left me with
Nothing...

He's holding that fear
Closer to his heart
Than you can imagine
He's holding you
Responsible
For those sleepless nights
He's leading others
To believe
That he's stronger
Stronger, than he's ever been
That fire you placed in him
Died, a long time ago.
He believes nothing
Will ever ruin him
Yet little does he know
His demons can never be tamed
All he has are those voices
That once sang, but now they scream
He's holding you
Responsible
For that Fire
He let die, a long time ago...

Because

The number one reason
I don't believe in God
Is because
No matter how many times
I've asked him to kill me...

He never did...

All I wanted was for someone to love me,
Like they were a shooting star
That's finally found its home...

Because

I need someone
To need me
When I don't even
Want myself...

Because you smiled
And said
Thanks for coming
And hugged me
As strangers do
And I just kinda sat
There and said
Yeah
But I wondered
Who the fuck
Did you think
You were talking to,
I held you when you were sick
I dried your tears
I fucking believed in you
When you didn't
For fuck sakes
You loved me once...

Because

I've found that I fall in love with people who are
just as broken as me. We try to fit out broken
pieces together, but were simply made from
different dreams...

Sometimes
I wish my monsters
Would scream
Because honestly
When they scream
There words
Aren't nearly
As beautiful
As when
They whisper
Sweet nothings
In my ear...

Because

Because
People will be people
And forget
That there
Are hearts
Inside of us...

I'd sell my soul to the devil ...

To be your kind of perfect....

Don't you get it?
I called you perfect
I planted that thought
Into your brain...

I watered you
Fed you

And watched you grow
Right the fuck
Out of my life

Because finally
I made you
Believe in something

You never were...

I didn't feel
For a moment
And in that
moment
I was terrified
Because
I feared
This nothingness
Would last
Forever...

Because

The rain reminds me
How lonely I am
It sends shivers down my spine
That hands will not comfort
The sound of the rain
Pounding the window
Will not be interrupted
By whispers of "I Love You"
In my ears
The coldness that
Invades my bed
Will not be replaced
By a warm loving soul
The rain reminds me
Of emptiness
And of
How lonely I am...

Until
I find someone
Who understands
Just how broken
I am
I will just be shiny pieces
Scattered
That you pick up
Keep for a while
Then toss back down...

Because

It's like we were polar opposites
I could never fit into
Your perfect existence
I was black and white
And you,
You were the god damn
Fucking Rainbow...

I just wonder
     What it's like
For someone
     To just once
Be Proud
     To call me theirs...

People like you
Are the reason
I can understand
Why I am not loved
You hate me to
My core yet,
You are my own
Flesh and Blood...

There are these moments
When life throws you
Into Hell
And you never think
You'll climb from the depths
But these are only moments,
Temporary moments
Just remember
Heaven is always in reach...

Because

Part of me
Will never understand
How someone
Would outcast
A person who
Built a bridge for you
Watched you burn it
And once the ashes settled
Built it again,
So that you know
You're always welcome
In my heart...

We're not all meant to fly
Bu you, you were meant
For so much more
You were meant
To soar....

Memories
Are what shatter the heart
Little moments
That continuously tear us apart
Down to mere seconds
It's a form of art
It's not the real thing
Only a part
I can't recall
If you were a dream
But maybe if you were
You were only meant to gleam
Shine, and glisten away into the night
Forever in my heart
But will you stay in my mind?
Just as you were
Or will I change you a bit?
Because you were far from perfect
But in my memory
You can be...

That road was empty
From the very start
And with the silence
Your heavy breathing
Echoed throughout the car
The trees grew closer
As we drifted apart
Who knew we'd
Go in together
And come out
Lonely hearts...

Because

Drowning
    Was never an option before...

        But drifting away at sea

            Until you're too tired
            To come back

                Seems more
                    Beautiful than ever...

You had the power
To turn everything
You touched into gold
Yet, you refused to touch me
In fear
I'd become everything
You both
Loved and loathed...

Because

Your drive to live
Has dwindled
Almost disappeared
You've become
Extremely frangible
In such a hostile world
And sometimes
I wonder
If you'll ever
Survive...

I never wanted to cry over you
I never wanted to give you that satisfaction
Because you never deserved
Any part of me
Especially the parts
I showed you...

Because

And it's like a wave
That keeps pulling you down
I've forgotten how to swim
This sadness is pulling me under
And this time
I know
I'm going to drown...

My fingertips
Cross your chest
And I can feel
Your heartbeat
Which miraculously
Matches my own
Because when I'm with you
There's no me
Only us...

Because

Before you
My nightmares
Were just that
Terrifying dreams
That jolted me awake
But after you
My nightmares
Were never the same
Because
Loving you
Was more terrifying
Then I'd ever
Like to think....

Stop reminding me
I'm not a princess
Because
My fairytale ending
Stayed true
To the tales
Just little did I know
My fairytale
Was written by
Grimm himself...

Because

This is it
This was all we were ever meant to be...
And part of me
Will never understand
How fate could be
So cruel...

I've become lost, looking for my wonderland. Looking for my place, where my horrid thoughts no longer crowd my mind. You see, I don't believe I've found my white rabbit. I think he's lost or better yet, running late. Because I've marked my calendar, I've saved a date, and nothing is more beautiful then deciding your own fate. I have no time for Hello's only Goodbye's so please, he's late, so late, too late...

I want to be so gone

That the Mad Hatter

Thinks I've gone too far

And Alice is a little jealous

I've fallen

Farther than Wonderland...

These Seasons

The summer breeze brushed the hair into my face, and you gently swept it aside, and in that moment I looked at him and I knew what people meant when they said, they could love someone forever. Finally, I could understand those feelings people said they could never put into words. I now knew what it felt like to smile effortlessly, to the point where I didn't even realize it. I wondered how someone so beautiful could love someone like me. Because of you everything was perfect.

And then...

The seasons changed and with the cold breeze of Autumn came the cold realization of affliction. Such a captivating season. The leaves became more vibrant as ever and you never realized how beautiful they actually are until they start falling. And as I watched that once warm summer breeze turn frigid as it swiftly carried those beautiful leaves away, I watched this disease plague your body. I watched him smile less often. I watched how it became painful for him to talk about forever. I now knew what it felt like to feel helpless. To realize that no matter what you do you can't take the pain away. I shuttered at the thought of how something so beautiful, had to come to an end. Because of you, I hated Autumn. I hated Autumn because I was scared.

And just like Autumn, I watched you fade.

That frigid breeze turned unforgiving. And just like that forever... ceased to exist. And just like everything during the winter, I was frozen. Those once beautiful trees, now dead. Everything seemed so sinister. Just like the winter air, the idea of never hearing you say my name again, made it nearly impossible to breathe. The snow was no longer fresh, I could no longer seem to find the beauty or relief in the dirty snow banks. Your pain was gone, but now my pain engulfed me. I feared winter would extirpate me, I feared winter would be my last season because finally I understood those feelings people said they could never put into words. I now knew what it felt like to cry effortlessly, to the point where I didn't even realize it. I wondered how someone so beautiful could be taken away from me. Because of you, I was numb.

Winter lasted for what seemed like forever, but at sometime everything must thaw.

I've always hated spring. I cry more than it rains. I now knew it was possible to effortlessly forget how to smile. The snow, begins to slowly disappear and small buds begin to appear on those dead, haunting trees. Yet the rain still hits my window. The sun became brighter and brighter as it began to shine into my room. Reminding me there's still beauty out there, but none like yours. I only wish to have that summer breeze, the summer breeze that I shared with you. You planted these memories in my mind, and I have to remember showers bring flowers. I remind myself, it can't rain forever, just as these tears will not fall forever, and happiness is in the distance. Because of you, I am hopeful.

And with time, the rain stopped.

That summer breeze swept under my door and invited me outside. The breeze pushed my hair into my face and I slowly swept it aside, and then there it was in all its beauty. Summer was here, and so were you. The trees tall and green, seemed as if they were dancing. They were free, from their crippling Autumn, liberated from their cold harsh winter. Just as you were. It took me all this time to realize that I could still have a forever. I felt the warm grass between my toes, Happiness, because finally I could attach words to my feelings. I effortlessly smiled, because though it's hard at times, it's still possible to smile. I inhaled and realized my breath didn't escape me. I could breathe. I could finally be free too. Because you were all my seasons, but you will always be my Summer.

And summer was beautiful...

Because

www.ingramcontent.com/pod-product-compliance
Lightning Source LLC
LaVergne TN
LVHW041214080426
835508LV00011B/958